LIGHTNING BOLT BOOKS™

What Is Smell?

Jennifer Boothroyd

Lerner Publications Company
Minneapolis

For Jacob

1/10

Lerner Publications Company
A division of Lerner Publishing Group, Inc.
241 First Avenue North
Minneapolis, MN 55401 U.S.A.

Website address: www.lernerbooks.com

Library of Congress Cataloging-in-Publication Data

What is smell? / by Jennifer Boothroyd.
     p.   cm. — (Lightning bolt books™ — Your amazing senses)
   Includes index.
   ISBN 978–0–7613–4253–3 (lib. bdg. : alk. paper)
   1. Smell—Juvenile literature. I. Title.
  QP458.B67 2010
  612.8′6—dc22   2008051850

Manufactured in the United States of America
1 2 3 4 5 6 — BP — 15 14 13 12 11 10

Contents

Gathering Information

Take a deep breath through your nose.

Did you smell anything?

Maybe you smelled cookies baking. Or the scent of rain through an open window.

Freshly baked cookies smell delicious!

Smelling is one of your five senses.

You use
your nose
to smell
things.

Your sense of smell helps you learn about the world. It can also protect you from danger.

Your sense of smell gives you lots of information about the world around you.

Your Nose

How does your nose sense a smell?

Scent particles travel from objects—such as these muffins—to your nose.

Most things release scent particles. Scent particles are invisible chemicals that drift from an object and into the air.

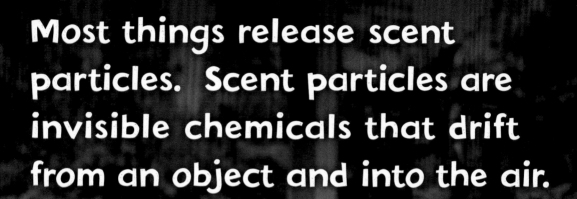

When you breathe,
your nose takes in
scent particles.

Special nerves in your nose change the particles into an electrical signal. The signal is sent to your brain.

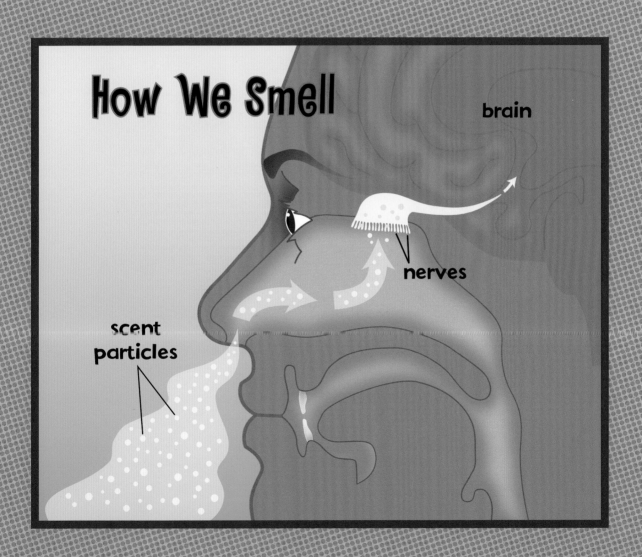

How We Smell

brain

nerves

scent particles

Your brain tells you if the smell is familiar and if it is good or bad.

The powerful smell of onions makes some people cry.

In the Air

A scent is strong if you are close to its source.

Food cooking on the stove smells the strongest in the kitchen.

Kitchens at dinnertime often smell strongly of food.

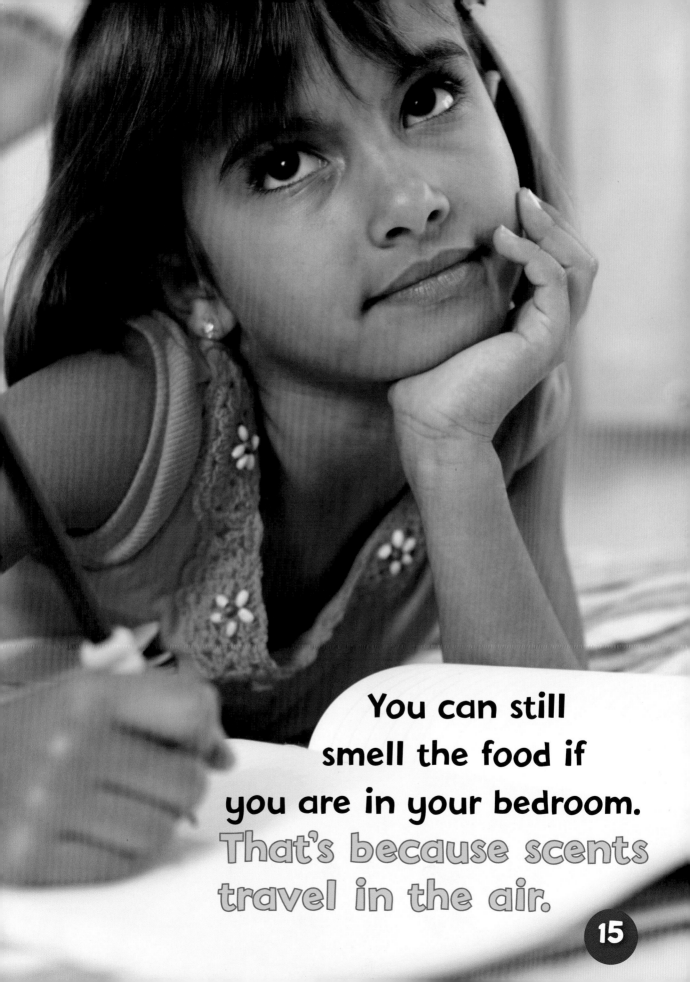

You can still smell the food if you are in your bedroom. That's because scents travel in the air.

But the smell won't be as strong as it is in the kitchen.

Good and Bad Smells

People can identify thousands of smells.

The human nose detects a huge variety of scents.

Some smells are nice.
Others are awful.

The smell of a cat's litter box may make you want to hold your nose!

Roses smell sweet.

Garbage cans stink.

A Matter of Opinion

Sometimes people disagree about smells.

Your mom
loves the
smell of
fresh coffee.

You may not.

Protection from Danger

Your sense of smell can protect you from danger.

Your nose can tell you if milk has gone sour or if meat has spoiled.

The rotten smell warns you not to eat the food.

Sour milk can make you sick. Its smell lets you know that it's not safe to drink.

The strong smell of smoke can let us know if there's a fire in a building. It says that we should leave right away and get help.

It's best to leave a building if it smells of smoke. It's also smart to tell an adult.

Smelling is
an important
sense. You use
it every day.

Activity

Test Your Sense of Smell

Ask an adult if you can try this experiment to test your sense of smell.

What you need:

any four of the following items:
- peppermint extract
- vanilla extract
- an orange slice
- coffee grounds
- vinegar
- garlic
- pine needles

four small plastic containers or cups

a friend or classmate to work with

a cloth to use as a blindfold

What you do:

1. Put each of your four items into a separate container or cup. Be sure to put enough of the item into the container so that you can smell the item.

2. Have your friend tie the cloth around your eyes.

3. Next have the friend hold each of the containers near your nose and see if you can guess which item you are smelling.

4. If you want, you can switch roles and see if your friend can guess which item he or she is smelling.

Glossary

chemical: a substance used in or produced by chemistry

invisible: something that cannot be seen

nerve: a thin fiber that sends messages between your brain and other parts of your body

opinion: the ideas and beliefs that you have about something

particle: a small piece or amount of something

scent: a smell or an odor

sense: one of the powers that people and animals use to learn about their surroundings. The five senses are sight, hearing, touch, taste, and smell.

source: the place or thing from which something comes

Further Reading

Enchanted Learning: Five Senses Theme Page
http://www.enchantedlearning.com/themes/senses
.shtml

Haddon, Jean. *Make Sense!* Minneapolis: Millbrook Press, 2007.

Hewitt, Sally. *Smell It!* New York: Crabtree, 2008.

Kids Health: How the Body Works
http://kidshealth.org/kid/htbw

Rotner, Shelley. *Senses in the City.* Minneapolis: Millbrook Press, 2008.

Rotner, Shelley. *Senses on the Farm.* Minneapolis: Millbrook Press, 2009.

Index

Photo Acknowledgments

The images in this book are used with the permission of: ©iStockphoto/Franky DeMeyer, pp. 1, 19; © Corbis/Photolibrary, p. 2; © Ichip/Dreamstime.com, p. 4; © age fotostock/Super-Stock, p. 5; © Felixcasio/Dreamstime.com, p. 6; Reflexstock/Zen Shui/Laurence Mouton, p. 7; Reflexstock/Corbis, pp. 8, 20;© Alan Hicks/Stone/Getty Images, p. 9; Reflexstock, p. 10; © Laura Westlund/Independent Picture Service, p. 11; Reflexstock/Blend/Hill Street Studios, p. 12; © Food Collection/Photolibrary, p. 13; © iStockphoto.com/Dutchy, p. 14;© Kraig Skarbinsky/Digital Vision/Getty Images, p. 15; © Betsy Van Der Meer/Taxi/Getty Images, p. 16; © iStockphoto.com/anzeletti, p. 17; © Chris Alvanas/Rubberball Productions/Getty Images, p. 18; © iStockphoto.com/Franky DeMeyer, p. 19; Reflexstock/Radius Images/Corbis, p. 21; © Garry Wade/Taxi/Getty Images, p. 22; © Mocker/Dreamstime.com, p. 23; Reflexstock/Stock Connection/Jagdish Agarwal, p. 24; © Gelpi/Dreamstime.com, p. 25; © Bob Rowan; Progressive Image/CORBIS, p. 26; © iStockphoto.com/eva serrabassa, p. 27; © Todd Strand/Independent Picture Service, p. 28; © iStockphoto.com/Cheryl Casey, p. 30; © iStockphoto.com/Joan Vincent Canto Roig, p. 31.

Front cover: © iStockphoto.com/Franz-W. Franzelin (gerbera daisy); © iStockphoto.com/MB-PHOTO (cherry pie); © Fedor Kondratenko/Dreamstime.com (silver fish).